Little Hedge King
© 2008 Daniele Luciano Moskal

UNIQUE WRITING PUBLICATIONS

ISBN 0-9545113-36

Unless otherwise indicated, all Scripture quotations are taken from the *King James Version* (KJV), of the Holy Bible.

All rights reserved. No part of this book may be reproduced or transmitted in any form or by any means, electronic or mechanical, including photocopying, recording, or by any information storage and retrieval system, without written permission from the publisher.

Contents

Dedication

Author's Note

Description of Wren

Crucifixion

St. Stephen's Day

Hunting the Wren

Why are so many people scared of spiders?

Scavenger of all Scavengers

Conclusion

Dedication

I dedicate this book to my One and Only Love - my Lord and personal Saviour Jesus Christ - who continues to inspire me with His divine supernatural inspiration to write unique teaching books in a simple yet easy-to-comprehend way, bringing glory and honour to His awesome, loving and faithful name.

Thank-you Holy Spirit, You are my wonderful teacher and spiritual guide who continues to guide me into all truth.

Thank-you Lord, for the anointed writing gifts You have bestowed and invested within me.

May the whole earth be filled with Your glory, as the waters cover the seas, in Jesus Christ's magnificent name!

To my special daughters

Temidayo & Carol-Jean

Author's Note

For as long as I can remember growing up as a young, bright-eyed, adventurous, skinny kid in Gainsborough, a small historical Lincolnshire town in England, with plenty of surrounding woodland, I have been fascinated with small Garden Birds (especially the '*Wren*'). This very small, diminutive bird is probably one of Britain's most widely distributed species, and certainly the cutest, I've ever had the privilege of observing on numerous occasions. In severe winters the population of this "*little hedge king*" bird , as I like to call the Wren, can be severely and drastically reduced but after a succession of recent mild winters here in England, it has now probably become one of Britain's commonest species of Garden Birds. The *"little hedge king"*, can also be found throughout Europe as well as in China, Japan, India and the United States, where it is known as the *'Winter Wren'*. It is unquestionably a highly intelligent, adaptable bird; there is hardly any habitat it has not colonised and is quite at home in gardens, woodlands, on rocky coasts or on mountain tops. You may be asking right now, why on earth I and so many folk around the world call this fascinating small bird *"little hedge king?"* I hope by simply reading this book you will understand the awesome reverence and somewhat mysterious personality and uncanny resemblance to the Christian Gospel of our Lord Jesus Christ of Nazareth, that this small but cute Garden Bird has brought to the lives of people throughout the world, including myself!!

From Evangelist Daniele Luciano Moskal (John3-34)

Description of Wren

The Wren (*Troglodytes Troglodytes* from the Greek meaning "one who creeps into holes") is a very small but stocky, restless bird that is easily recognised by its brown plumage and short cocked tail which they continuously flick repeatedly. The upper parts and flanks have dark barring and the pale eyebrow (supercilium) is prominent. The under parts are paler with grey barring. The bill is brownish and the legs are fleshy-brown. Juvenile wrens look similar to adults but their eyebrow may not be as prominent until they get their adult plumage. In flight, the wren wing beats are rapid and it usually flies short distances and in a straight line. The wren weighs

approximately the weight of a British £1 coin and lives life at a fast, restless pace and it sings this way too - it trembles as it puts everything into its song, which lasts about 5 seconds and usually ends in a trill. Subsequently, what this bird lacks in size, it more than makes up for in voice and chances are that you will hear its amazingly loud song before you see it!!

Their alarm call is a loud "*teck-teck-teck*". When feeding, wrens eat spiders and insects which they find while hopping and dashing along the ground and probing in crevices with their long thin bill. When they do venture out into the open they dart from one place to another. When nesting wrens will use open-fronted and tit nest boxes, both for nesting and winter roosting (up to 60 have been recorded in one box).

The male bird constructs several globe-shaped nests in holes in walls, banks, trees, or old nests from leaves, grass and moss. When the female has chosen a nest, she lines it with feathers.

The smooth, glossy eggs are white with reddish spots, and about 16 mm by 13 mm. Incubation is by the female only. The young are continuously fed by both

parents. Most British wrens are sedentary though some move up to 250 km (150 miles) into more sheltered habitats, such as reed beds, for the winter. European wrens are both sedentary and migratory - the latter flying anything up to 2500 km (1500 miles).

The ***"little hedge king"*** is not only

one of my favourite species of Garden Bird but it seems to be very popular with many country folk not only in England, but in Scotland, Wales, Ireland, France, Italy - almost all over Europe. Apparently, for many years it has been given a majestic title *"king", "little king", "hedge king",* and other fine names.

In the West of England, through the centuries people have been heard saying these words:

> **"Whosoever kills a robin or a wren,**
> **Shall never prosper boys or men."**

In Scotland young boys sing or used to sing this song:

> **"Malisons, malisons, mair than ten,**
> **That harry the Ladye of Heaven's hen."**

Apparently, the reason for the singing of this Scottish song was that whosoever robbed the eggs from the nest of this tiny bird which was supposed to be under the care and protection of Jesus Christ's mother - the Virgin Mary - curses would be upon them. In some parts of England, I've heard many fascinating tales and mysteries in particular from the older generation concerning this *"little hedge king"*. It is believed my many folk that anyone who kills a wren or harries its nest, will either break a bone, or come to some other serious trouble before the year ended. Some men and women even thought that the popular black & White, Friesian cows would all produce blood instead of milk!

I discovered only recently that even in France at one place in Brittany, parents would tell their children that if they touched the young wrens in their nest they would suffer terribly from the fire of St. Lawrence - that pimples would spread all over their face, arms, back and legs!

 How this tiny diminutive bird, of approximately 3 - 4 inches in length came to be so reverentially feared and honoured, has fascinated me for years. Perhaps, it's something to do with its tremendous courage when it has such tiny young fledglings to defend, or its unique cleverness in nest-building, or the cunning wisdom with which the male bird makes sham nests so as to lead the predator nest-hunter astray, may have gained respect for it; but this is only few things to keep you guessing.

Hunting the Wren

One of the strangest facts I've recently discovered about the treatment of the *"little hedge king",* is that, once a year, the wren bird which is held in reverence for nearly all the other part of the twelve calendar months is mostly cruelly used. In many places, years ago, it was the custom to go *"hunting the wren"*. In the Isle of Man it was customary in bygone days to do so on Christmas morning. On December 24th, towards evening, all the servants of the wealthy homes would be off on holiday; they did not go to bed all night, but rambled about till the church bells rang out their melodious song at midnight. When prayers and the short sermon were over, they went to *"hunt the wren"* and having found one of these birds, they killed it, and fastened it to the top of a long pole with its wings extended. Thus they carried it in procession to every house in the district, chanting the following rhyme:

> *"We hunted the wren for Robin the Bobbin,*
> *We hunted the wren for Jack of the Can;*
> *We hunted the wren for Robin the Bobbin,*
> *We hunted the wren for everyone."*

As a Christian, I can somewhat relate this above scene to that of Jesus Christ of Nazareth praying in the Garden of Gethsemane before Judas *'the betrayer'*, the Temple Guards and Roman soldiers came to arrest Jesus, at midnight, to that of *"The little hedge king"* - my *'king'* of all the garden birds.

I don't know if you can see what I am definitely seeing concerning the picture of the wren, but somehow I can uncannily relate the body of this innocent small bird being torn apart - its delicate wings stretched and exposed, is very similar to Jesus' arms being extended from their joints on the Cross at Calvary Hill. I can relate also to all the chants of the island's servants on December 24th - to the Easter period in history 2,000 years ago, when Jesus Christ of Nazareth's body - was hung and crucified on a rugged beam - like that of the wren being fastened to the servant's pole - with the mocking, jeering, cheering, wicked chants of religious leaders and intellectual men of their day cursing Him, wishing Him dead. Yes, I can even relate this account to Isaiah's prophetic vision found and recorded in Chapter 53 of his book in the Old Testament of the Holy Bible, where the prophet describes Jesus Christ as the *"Suffering servant",* an innocent, harmless, sacrificial Lamb that was led to the slaughter and to these two Scripture verses, were Jesus Himself speaking to His disciples about His death and resurrection in the **Book of Matthew 21:18-19 (KJV).**

18 " Behold, we go up to Jerusalem; and the Son of man, shall be betrayed unto the chief priests and unto the scribes, and they shall condemn him to death,

19 And shall deliver him to the Gentiles to mock, and to scourge, and to *<u>crucify</u>* him: and the third day he shall rise again.

Crucifixion

This was a method widely used in Biblical times. The victim was hung on a cross made of two wooden beams, one horizontal the other vertical and left there to die a most brutal, painful, agonising slow death. Jesus Christ of Nazareth's crucifixion is the most famous in all history. Jesus allowed the Romans to kill him because it fulfilled God's plan, bringing salvation to sinners. Jesus' painful death on a cross made it possible for everyone who believes in him to be forgiven of their sins and accepted by God. The term *"cross"* is also used in the Holy Bible in a symbolic way. Jesus used it to describe the kind of sacrifice that His followers must be willing to make. Similarly, the Apostle Paul used it to stand for the death of self that takes place when a Christian becomes more and more like Christ.

Long before Jesus Christ died, crucifixion was used by many different peoples to punish their criminals and enemies.
A few hundred years before the time of Jesus of Nazareth, the Medes and Persians were apparently the first people to practice crucifixion. Crucifixion was also used by other nations who lived around the Mediterranean Sea: the Greeks, the Carthaginians, and closer to the time of Jesus, the Romans.

These people used different kinds of crosses. Sometimes a person would be impaled on a sharp, pointed stick planted in the ground. (The Greek word for *"cross"* means *"stake")*. More often, a person would be hung on a cross that was formed either in the shape of a capital **T** or in the shape we are more familiar with the crossbeam attached partway down the upright beam.

Crucifixion was seen everywhere as the most horrible type of execution. For that reason, the Greeks and Romans used it only for slaves and foreigners, not for their own citizens. Other peoples would hang victims on crosses only after they had died by some more merciful form of execution. The Romans generally performed their crucifixions this way:

First, the victim was severely whipped with a whip that had approximately nine long leather tails, containing small pieces of sharp bone or sharp metal at the end of their tails that would literally tear the flesh from the victim's body, exposing their bones in most cases. Then he was forced to carry the crossbeam to the spot where the crucifixion was to take place. There he was either tied or nailed to the crossbeam, with the nails driven through his wrists. Next, the crossbeam (with the victim hanging from it) was raised and fixed to an upright pole. A sign describing the crime was sometimes hung around the victim's neck or attached to his cross. The victim's ankles were sometimes nailed to the upright pole. If the executioners wanted to make the suffering last longer, a small seat or a support for the victim's feet was provided. A person crucified in this way eventually died from incredible blood loss or suffocation from hanging in such an awkward position. Sometimes the dying process took days. If the executioners wanted to hasten the death, they broke the victim's legs with a club. Once the victim was dead, his body was usually left on the cross to rot, although sometimes it would be given to relatives for burial. The Holy Bible tells us a lot about Jesus' death by crucifixion because it was the main reason He came to earth. Because of Jesus

Christ's death, His followers have the chance to be accepted by God. Christ's crucifixion and resurrection are the most important events recorded in the Holy Bible and central to a believer in Christianity. This all goes to show that Christ's crucifixion is crucial not only for how anyone who truly believes Jesus Christ died and rose again on the third day to begin a relationship with God, but also for how we live it throughout our lives. Nothing is more important for a Christian than the death of Jesus Christ.

St. Stephen's Day

Approximately in the middle of the past century boys also went from door to door on St. Stephen's Day (December 26th) with a wren suspended by the legs in the centre of two hoops which crossed each other at right angles, and were decorated with evergreens and ribbons. The bearers would sing lines about boiling and eating the bird. If at the close of the song they received a small coin, they would give in return a feather from the bird, so that before the end of the day the wren hung almost featherless. It was then buried on the seashore, or in some waste place. The people who had received the feathers took the greatest care of them, as it was believed that to possess one was a sure preservative from any shipwreck for a whole year, and a fisherman who didn't get one was thought to be very foolish.

The custom of *"hunting the wren"* was unfortunately still kept up many years ago in some parts of Ireland - namely Leinster and Connaught - and used to be observed in England and in France. **(Personally speaking I must stress the fact that I have not come across one single recorded case in the writing and finishing of this book).**

Unfortunately, many of our forefathers many, many, years ago probably used to worship beasts, reptiles and birds in one form or another. It is a long, long, time ago since our forefathers worshipped animals, and yet a custom that was part of their worship has only just come to my knowledge died out of the British Isles not many years ago - *"hunting the wren"*. Today, there are people in this world who grumble at our

Christian outreach workers, missionaries and church leaders, because they don't quickly succeed in persuading heathen folk to give up all their superstitions and idolatrous ways, and here you see that we as enlightened people (as most of us think about ourselves), kept up a piece of idolatry worship till yesterday almost. I believe we must have a lot more patience with all the Christian organisations, and their converts after that, I think!

Now seeing that we have got rid of the cruel and senseless practice of *"hunting the wren"*, could it be possible that there may be other such animal practices still prevailing in life today which would be better if we totally abandoned?

Although the wren was hunted only once a year; all the rest of the twelve months it was treated with respect. How I wish by the grace and mercy of God that people everywhere around the world - young or old - black or white - would remember not just for a day Jesus' sacrificial death on the Cross at Calvary, but for twelve months a year , every year?!!

Yes, there was little excuse for the fisherman who was glad that the hunt had been successful, because after all he had a charm, a wren's feather, that would keep him safe from shipwrecks for a year - so he believed, and somehow we always seem to make excuses for honest believers, even when their belief is not wise.

Subsequently, it wasn't so long ago that thousands and thousands of birds were hunted not once a year, but all the year around, so that their wings and feathers could be stuck upon the heads of British women and girls. Many of the wings which were torn off the bodies were of living birds, because it was believed that the feathers kept their colour when this was done. Maybe you didn't know that tens of thousands of beautiful innocent creatures were annually tortured and killed, just so that their dead limbs could be worn by gentle fashionable ladies of their day.

Conclusion

Whether you are a Christian or non-Christian, I hope that you as the reader of this book can see for yourself the uncanny but striking similarity of the *"little hedge king"*, and somehow resemble it to the Crucifixion of the true **"King of Kings" - our LORD and Saviour Jesus Christ of Nazareth.**

Just like the innocent small wren was hunted down, crucified for fun, killed by many folk and placed on a pole with its wings appalling stretched from its featherless body for all to see and mock, so too was Jesus Christ an innocent Jewish Rabbi hunted down by the religious fraternity of His day 2,000 years ago and met a cruel death, where His naked and bloody flesh was exposed for all humanity on a rugged cross at Calvary Hill, in

Israel. Once again, we have recorded proof like that of *"hunting the wren"* of how long some ancient customs have lived. One reason of this is that we seem to keep on doing things simply because we have done them before, or because other people still do so. But if we could ask ourselves in all honesty whether our actions are morally right, wise, or kind to people in everyday real-life issues, then there would be many good things, not a few, which would quickly go out of fashion as completely as the *"hunting of the wren"* - my **("little hedge king")** - and the world would undoubtedly be a much better place to live in!!

Why are so many people frightened of spiders?

And why do so many of us think household spiders are " nasty, horrible, sinister, creepy-crawly things", and don't care to study them or learn from them; that they are only here on earth to be trod upon, slapped with a newspaper, sprayed, killed, or simply to be avoided at all costs? I hope to prove to you that they are neither nasty, horrid, sinister, creepy crawlies, but very intelligent, interesting creatures. Certainly, if we admire cleverness, patience, courage, affection, we must admire spiders – for they have all these qualities in a very high degree.

But why do so many people, young and old absolutely hate them? They cannot sting you as wasps can; they cannot bite you as several kinds of flies can; they do no harm to the flowers and fruit we grow in our gardens as earwigs, caterpillars and ants do; they don't meddle with the food and sweets we store in our cupboards or kitchens (as mice or rats do if the opportunity arises); they do not give plagues to horses or cows, sheep or dogs, as some insects do. NO! Spiders injure nothing which belongs to us. So far as I am concerned they are perfectly innocent creatures. But they catch poor flies you may shout! Is this the reason why so many of us loathe them and think them nasty and horrible?

Do you think fishermen are because they catch poor fish? Do you think the same of hunters in other parts of the world – who trap and kill innocent animals? I hope you are not disgusted with swallows and the other birds which catch flies on the wing, are you? As for me, I am rather grateful to the creatures that keep the swarms of flies in check a little; if it were not for spiders the flies would drive man and beast to madness or death. I don't believe in all honesty that the secret of your dislike to spiders is that they capture and eat a few flies. I also incline to believe that they have too many legs to please you. There aren't't many animals known to me or you which have eight legs, and such legs as those of a spider. I may be wrong however, but I fancy it might be the unusual number of limbs and the unusual manner of walking that make some people afraid of the harmless spiders.

If you just try to get over your phobia or aversion so far as to watch the ways and doings of spiders, I am very sure you will be full of surprise and wonder at their sheer cleverness.

For instance, you may wake up early one morning and go into

your garden (for those of us who have gardens), and look for a Geometrical Spider making or mending her web in a bush. I will not spend time in trying to describe for you how she goes about her work, for you will learn very much more by observing with your own eyes for five to ten minutes than you could by reading for an hour.

If you go out into the country to a field and examine the gorse bushes on a summer's day, you may see another weaving spider, which makes a bower for herself and a chamber for her eggs.

There are many kinds of spiders to be found in Great Britain, seven hundred or more. Not all of them are web-makers. Some of them lie in wait, and spring upon their prey; some chase and run it down. But you will most easily find and watch some of the weaver spiders, and the closer you look at them the more reason I believe you will find to respect Mistress Spider for her clever skills and patience. Perhaps you may like to hear of what I saw a little while ago. A big fly entangled himself in the web which a small spider had made in one of the panes of my greenhouse, and the owner the (spider) rushed out in a great hurry. Here was perhaps the first chance of a meal that she had had for days, so although the trapped fly was "big game", and struggled strongly to free himself, she ventured up to him and began to tie him fast. In approximately a minute, however, he broke loose, but he fell into another web spun across the pane below. The Mistress of this web, Spider Number Two let us call her, hastened to seize the booty, and Number One Spider came to her help. Between them they managed to secure the fly.

Then they faced each other, and I suppose they argued the question as to which of them the game belonged to – with their eyes at any rate. Suddenly, Number One made a rush at Number Two, who retired to her lair, and Number One sat down to dinner. Number Two Spider made three attempts to share the meal, but was driven away every time. When she made the fourth attempt, Number One pursued her further than before, and then ran round the upper part of the web, and tore up the cords by which Number Two could come to disturb her. Then she dined in peace and quietness, but she took much less time over the meal than I expected and went off to her own premises. Then Number Two repaired a broken line, and came to take what was left. Do you see how much good sense was shown? Intelligence is mostly tested by unforeseen and uncommon circumstances. How seldom it must happen that a half-caught fly falls out of one web directly into another? How quickly the two spiders were to perceive that they ought to join their efforts! How swiftly Number One saw that the best way to prevent Number Two from interfering with her over her dinner was to cut off the communicating cords!

I am quite satisfied that Number One left part of the booty for the use of Number Two, proving that she has sense of what was just. But as you did not see the business, and perhaps don't notice spiders as much as I do, you may be right to doubt that. But I hope you saw the good judgment and prompt decision? And if you think how often a spider must have to use judgment, in the ordinary way of her work in making and mending her net as well as in dealing with different kinds of game, you will be greatly astonished that she is prepared for action in new and extraordinary circumstances. You may be asking yourself, why I have said "she" in talking about spiders. Because it is the lady spider only who spins and weaves the web; the gentleman (of that tribe), do nothing but entertain and amuse the ladies! It is quite true, and one of the ways in which they please their wives is by **DANCING.** Dancing is an accomplishment of several kinds of spiders, and good, trustworthy observers have funny tales to tell of their time spent watching the gentlemen performing for a length of time, bowing and bending, and twirling round until the lady is induced to become a partner in the waltz. You may be disposed to ask whether spiders are fond of music as well as dancing. So some say who have studied their ways. Solitary prisoners I have been told have drawn spiders from their holes and their nests just by whistling. Spiders have let themselves down by a single cord from the ceiling when a violin was being played, and fled back upwards at a great rate when the full orchestra crashes in. "Oh", say some, "the spider takes the whistle or the sound of the violin for the buzz of a fly; that is why it comes out." But that won't do at all, for this plain reason: you cannot draw a spider out of its hiding-place by a real buzz.

She never wastes her time in looking after insects which are not in her web. There are many interesting facts to be told, but I will mention only one more. Spider mothers are most affectionate and courageous. They enclose their eggs in a silk purse; often a very charming bit of fancywork is involved. This purse

Mamma-Spider hangs from a grass-stalk in a shady place, or hides it under the bark of a tree, or otherwise puts it out of harm's way. She always remains close by to guard her treasure, and while she is protecting it, she ceases to be a timid creature. I have personally picked up such an egg pouch, and Mamma has almost flown to save it. She clung to it as I held it up, until I shook her off. Then she lay motionless, but when I restored her precious bag, she hurried away and tried to hide it in a new crevice. Some spiders take care of their little ones until they have grown big enough to go out in the world to fend for themselves. What do you think the young spiders live on? For some time they take nothing but dew. Spiders are always thirsty creatures, but in their early days of their lives they find their whole nourishment in water. I hope you have learned that spiders are something else – much more than nasty, horrible, creepy-crawlies. Do you remember the wise man who wrote this proverb?

"The spider lives in King's palaces."

And she is as wonderful as anything that can be found there!!!

THE SCAVENGER OF ALL SCAVENGERS
(Pagurus Bernhardus)

 The Hermit crab is probably one of the most fascinating and comical creatures you could ever wish to find or study. All though that is his most common name, and perhaps the best, he is often called the Soldier Crab, because he is given to fighting with his own species. However the scientific people, who normally dignify everything concerning which the talk about, would call him a *Pagurus Bernhardus*, a typical species of the Anomorous Crustaceans. The majority of sea

fishermen know him as the Jack-crab, and use him often as bait. Probably you have come across him no doubt on the shore, with his body concealed in a whelk shell, and his biggest claw covering the opening very neatly; or you may have seen him crawling along the bottom of a rock pool nimbly enough, only to see him retreating into his borrowed shell, and blocking up the entrance at the very first sign of danger with his big claw. If you have ever witnessed a hermit crab when the water was rather rough, you must have been tempted to laugh at the way in which he grabs and grasps at anything that resembles an anchor, and If you have seen him when he just so happened to be without a shell, you must have laughed at his comical appearance of his feeble and shrunken fourth and fifth pair of legs, and of the soft underbelly part of his body.

He seems to know that he cuts a most ridiculous figure, and he probably also knows what a helpless, unprotected plight he is in, for he will make haste to find and empty shell. And when he has found one, he pokes into it with his claws, and lifts it up as though he were weighing it. Once he is satisfied that it will make a suitable covering, he then whisks himself into it with great speed, making himself so fast and firm by a ridge on his back and the two little hooks at his tail, that if you and I attempted to pull him out we would undoubtedly tear him in two.

But sometimes he must let go of his hold, especially when a sea anemone may seize his shell, and then, he must vacate his home, if he can before she has him trapped, shell and all, in her entangling and poisonous threads; or a wave may dash him against a stone, and break his shell to pieces; or he may become too large for his habitation, and be as uncomfortable as a knight in armour that is way too small for him. Many people have commented that it is a rather miserable sort of life for a crab. Most crabs are, in general, such active, hardy fellows, strongly shielded by their own natural shells, and some of them have been known to swim many miles out to sea in quest of their meat. What a pitiful creature this hermit crab is, who must cover and protect his soft body with a shell that doesn't even belong to him, and hide himself in any hole he can find, and eat such food that just happens to be thrown his way! Unfortunately he is reduced to this. No crabs are very particular what they eat, I believe, but what other crabs disdain is good enough for the hermit. He is a capital scavenger in an aquarium because he is ready to devour all the orts and scraps which the other creatures leave.

How does this Anomorous Crustacean get to be such a poor creature?

The scientists are quite convinced that it is through laziness. Many years ago, his ancestors had a strong, shelly coat, like the more respectable crabs, and all their legs were adapted for walking or swimming, but they did not like too much exertion, so they lay in holes and under stones, taking large amounts of food as they could with very little effort. So a lazy father crab succeeded a lazy son crab, for generation after generation, and so gradually Nature allowed the hard, horny "Chi tine" or armour to wear away. She would not be at the pains to provide what was not put to use. Then it wan't long after some forefather of the hermit took to covering

himself with an empty shell, and the bad example was followed by his descendents, and in consequence, the fourth an fifth pair of legs being huddled up and cramped, bean to dwindle to the absurd limbs they have now become. It is Nature's law:

"If you will not use your powers, then you must lose them!"

It is her law for the limbs of a man as well as those of a hermit crab; it is her law for the limbs of the mind as well as for the limbs of the body. Whatever we desire to keep of the things she has given us we must simply use. I need not say more about that. In the case of the hermit crab, we see can see the reward of laziness. He does not lack courage, or at least pugnacity, but he is idle. But so wise is God that He turns the hermit's laziness to account - not for himself, but for us and other creatures. The crabs devour stuff which would make it near enough impossible for you to enjoy a visit to the seaside, which would drive away the people who live there; and out of all the species of crabs the hermit has the least dainty appetite. As he will not get his living actively, he is condemned to be called a *"scavenger of scavengers"*. I don't believe you could have any better warning of the evil of laziness or a better example of the wisdom which even idlers use than that of the scavenger of all scavengers - the incredible hermit crab!!

"Little Hedge King"
© 2008 Daniele Luciano Moskal

Books written by Daniele Luciano Moskal

Jesus His-story, UNEXPLAINABLE yet UNDENIABLE

Prayers of the Old Testament

Many are called but few are chosen

Fragile Handle with Care

I must 'Be-About' My Father's Business

If you would like to contact **Evangelist Daniele Luciano Moskal** concerning any of his books or his ministries, you can do so by sending him an email at this address: *penofareadywriter@hotmail.co.uk*

www.ingramcontent.com/pod-product-compliance
Lightning Source LLC
Chambersburg PA
CBHW041812040426
42450CB00001B/10